essential careers™

A CAREER AS A

MASON

EDWARD WILLETT

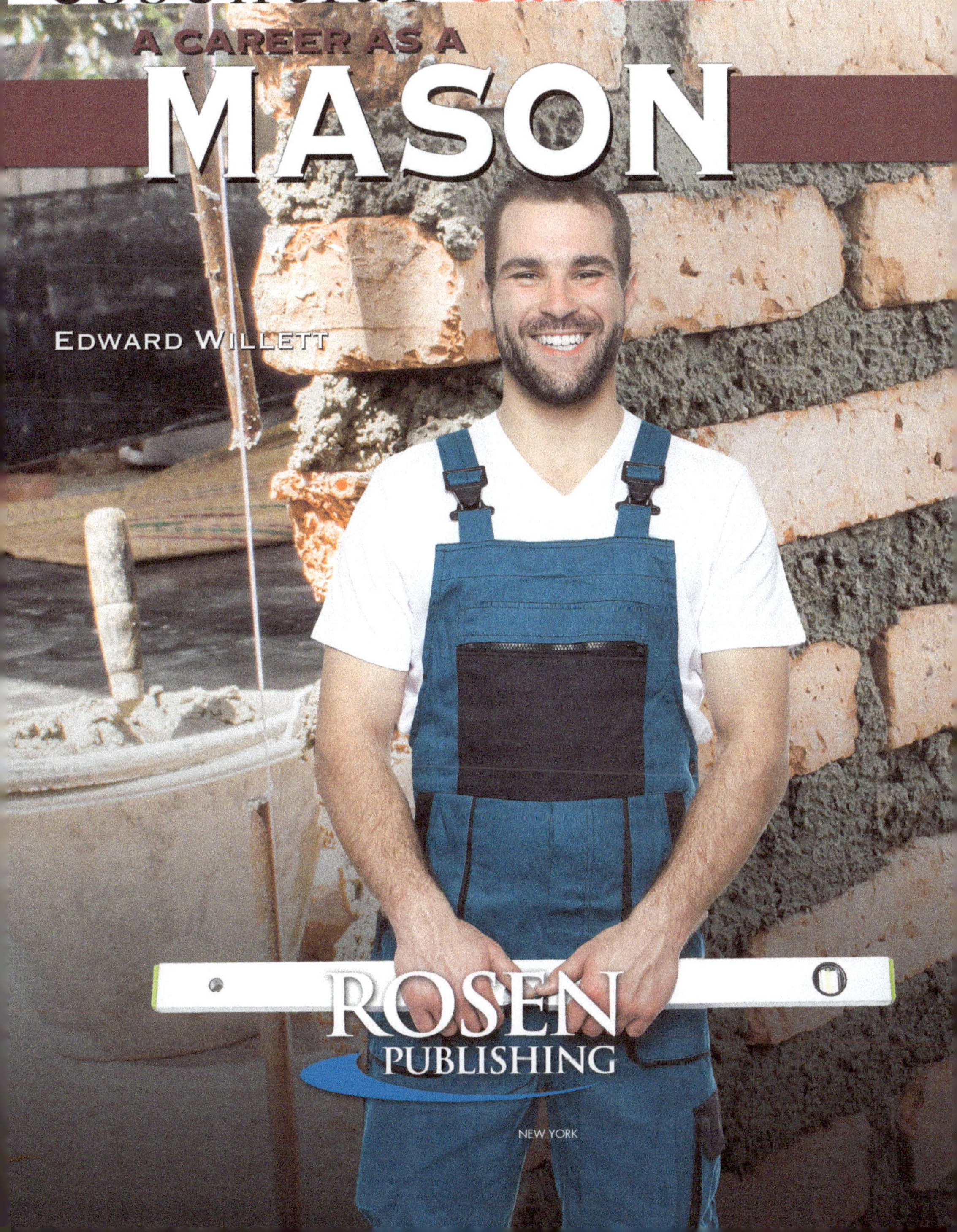

ROSEN
PUBLISHING
NEW YORK

Published in 2016 by The Rosen Publishing Group, Inc.
29 East 21st Street, New York, NY 10010

First Edition

Library of Congress Cataloging-in-Publication Data

Willett, Edward, 1959- author.
A career as a mason / Edward Willett. — First edition.
pages cm. — (Essential careers)
Includes bibliographical references and index.
ISBN 978-1-4994-6217-3 (library bound)
1. Masonry—Vocational guidance—Juvenile literature. I. Title. II. Series: Essential careers.
TH5321.W55 2016
693›.1023—dc23

2015024810

Manufactured in the United States of America

contents

INTRO

Bricks, used by humans for millennia, continue to be one of the world's most common building materials and are frequently used by masons.

DUCTION

Very few careers can be said to be as old as civilization. Most thrive for a time, then dwindle away as society changes. As a result, many careers that once provided employment for a large number of people no longer exist. For example, there aren't very many people making wagon wheels anymore, and in most towns, you'd be hard-pressed to find a blacksmith.

Some careers, however, seem to be able to weather the changing winds of time just fine. And one of those seemingly eternal careers, as old as history itself, is masonry.

The basic skill of masonry is bricklaying, and bricks are one of humanity's oldest building materials. The mud brick was invented sometime between 10000 and 8000 BCE. The molded brick (meaning all the bricks were made in a mold, making them all the same size and shape) came along in Mesopotamia about 5000 BCE. And the "modern" brick, made of fired clay, dates back to about 3500 BCE. Stone is another material used by ancient masons. Stonemasonry shares many similarities with brick masonry.

When you look back through history, you see that many of the greatest structures were made by masons. The ancient Romans used brick. The great church of Hagia Sophia, in Istanbul, is made of brick. In China, the largest man-made structure ever constructed, the Great Wall, is made of brick. The pyramids of Giza in Egypt are made of stone.

Millions and millions and millions of bricks have been used over the centuries to build these amazing structures and many more. Every one of those monumental achievements made use of craftspeople skilled at the job that has become known as "mason."

Masons today are an essential part of the construction industry. Many have mastered more than just bricks. They also work with concrete blocks, stone blocks, tiles, and many other materials, used every day in the construction of homes, businesses, and public buildings. Masons build walls and walkways, driveways and door arches, facades, and fireplaces. And although automated bricklaying robots are beginning to be developed, they must still be supervised by experienced masons and are limited in the kinds of work they can do.

Demand for masons is expected to grow far more quickly than for many other occupations over the next few years. No occupation is completely recession-proof, but a growing population means many new buildings will need to be constructed, and many of those buildings require masonry. Not only that, many older brick buildings are of historical value, and as they age, there is a need for skilled masons to restore and maintain these structures.

Best of all, for those with the aptitude and a willingness to work hard, the route to becoming a bricklayer is wide open. The requirements are straightforward: a high-school diploma, perhaps a year or two of technical training in a vocational institute, and three or four years of on-the-job training as an apprentice.

If you have good hand-eye coordination, physical strength and stamina, and decent math skills, this age-old profession could be the trade for you.

chapter 1

THE DEVELOPMENT OF MASONRY AND ITS ESSENTIAL MATERIALS

In 1952, an international team of archaeologists led by Kathleen Kenyon was excavating the ancient city of Jericho, on the banks of the River Jordan. Nothing remained of the city but a large mound, or tell, formed by the ruins of thousands of years of settlements piled up on one another. As the excavations continued, the archaeologists realized that the Jericho tell contained the remains of one of the oldest human settlements ever discovered, dating back to the Neolithic Period—also known as the Stone Age. That made it older than even the development of pottery or the discovery of metals.

But even though the ancient inhabitants hadn't figured out how to make fired clay pots, they'd learned how to make something else: bricks. The ancient towns preserved in the lowest levels of the Jericho tell were made of mud bricks. The oldest, which came from between 8300 and 7600 BCE, were shaped like loaves of bread. They were apparently made by scraping mud from the ground using a stick, mixing it with water, and then kneading and forming it by hand. The mud bricks were then dried by the sun and, once hard, were used to build thick walls, with more mud used as the mortar (the stuff that makes bricks stick together).

Many ancient buildings, like this one in Bani, Seno, Burkina Faso (West Africa), were built using bricks made of nothing more than dried mud.

The people who built those first brick walls were the world's first masons. Although the Jericho bricks are the oldest yet discovered, there is reason to believe they were being used in other parts of the ancient world at the same time and probably had been for centuries. Although such ancient structures reflect the importance of environment and climate in the development of the tools and equipment employed in masonry historically, the essential equipment—bricks, stone, and concrete—remain crucial even today in all types of surroundings around the world.

A New Technology

The trouble with hand-molded mud bricks was that they varied a lot in shape and size, which made it hard to fit them together smoothly. Their other shortcoming was that they were fitted together with nothing more than more mud. The mud was actually weaker than the bricks themselves, which made walls and other structures fragile and liable to collapse.

Still, for centuries, mud bricks were state-of-the-art, and the only improvement was the introduction of chopped straw and grass to the mud, which prevented distortion and cracking. That changed with the development of molded bricks, which became common in Mesopotamia between about 5900 and 5300 BCE. Brick molds helped standardize the size and shape of bricks, making them easier to use and fit together.

Those first known molded bricks are older than the discovery of metals, so it's a bit of a mystery how the molds were made. Molds are made of shaped wood. However, while it's easy to shape wood with a metal saw, it's a lot harder to shape it with the kinds of stone tools Neolithic people had. Joining the flat pieces of wood together to make the mold would also have been difficult.

So although we know the Mesopotamians were able to make molded bricks—because we can see the bricks—we don't

The Egyptians used brick molds like this one, found at the site of the Temple of Hathor, to make the bricks with which they built some of the greatest structures of the ancient world.

know how they did it. The oldest surviving brick molds date to much, much later—to the Egyptians.

ANOTHER INNOVATION

After the development of the molded brick, but long before the Egyptians started painting pictures of brickmaking on tomb walls, came another great technological change: the invention of fired bricks.

Bricks came before pottery, but once ancient people realized they could make clay much harder and water-resistant by

MOLDING BRICKS IN ANCIENT EGYPT

Rekh-mi-Re was vizier of Egypt in c. 1450 BCE. When he died, he was buried in a grand tomb in the city of Thebes. Festooning the walls of his tomb are the oldest surviving images of workmen using molds to make bricks.

The pictures show workers getting water from pools and brickmakers mixing it with mud and straw and then pushing the mixture into open-bottomed wooden molds on the ground. The clay sticking up above the top of the mold was scraped with a piece of wood to flatten it, and then the mold was lifted off and placed elsewhere on the ground to bake in the hot Egyptian sun while a new brick was made. A single brickmaker could make hundreds of identical rectangular bricks in a day with a mold.

Though the Egyptians did not invent molded bricks, they figured out exciting new things to do with them. One of the most important innovations of Egypt's skilled masons was the use of bricks to make arches and vaults, something they never did with stone.

firing it (heating it to a high temperature in a fire), it must have occurred to them pretty quickly that they could do the same thing to bricks. The oldest fired bricks discovered, dating to between 5000 and 4500 BCE, come from Mesopotamia, where they were used to make a drain. They seemed to be very rare, however, until a later period in history, between 3100 and 2900 BCE. Since the mud brick had been known for 5,000 years at that point, and pottery for 4,000, it may seem odd they weren't in wider use.

However, the likely reasons are pretty simple: in hot climates, mud bricks work well enough, and they're much cheaper.

Even today, mud bricks are the most common building material in the world. They are so easy to make (you don't really need any special skills to make a roughly rectangular mud brick, or even a molded one) that anyone who wants to build a house can make them himself or herself, given a supply of mud.

A fired brick—which is what we in the developed world tend to think of first when we think of bricks—has to first be made of clay and then heated to a temperature between 1740 and 2100 degrees Fahrenheit (950 and 1150 degrees Celsius). The temperature must be carefully controlled. If the clay gets too hot, the brick will melt into a glass-like blob, and if the clay doesn't get hot enough, the brick will be too fragile to be useful in building.

The ruins of elaborate structures like these in the ancient city of Ostia show that the Romans were masters of brick-making and bricklaying.

Because there was no way to tell if the right temperature was reached until after the firing was complete, it was easy to waste a lot of valuable fuel (often in short supply in primitive cultures) only to end up with something unusable. Selecting the right kind of clay also took special knowledge.

All of that meant that fired bricks, even centuries after they'd been invented, were far more expensive than mud bricks. In fact, according to a record from the Third Dynasty of Ur (2111–2003 BCE) from ancient Sumer, one piece of silver at the time would buy 14,400 mud bricks but only 504 fired bricks. To put it another way, fired bricks were thirty times more expensive than mud bricks. Even much later, when the Babylonians were making bricks in bulk, fired bricks cost two to five times more than mud bricks. (The Babylonians also developed the trick of adding glazes to brick: thin slurries of clay that, when fired, became brilliantly colored glass-like coverings, like the glaze on a piece of pottery.)

Yet fired bricks were clearly superior to mud bricks, too—waterproof and far stronger. That fact, combined with their cost, meant that the skilled masons who learned to work with them were mostly employed making temples and palaces. Ordinary buildings still made do with the cheaper and less durable mud bricks.

Brickmaking and the use of bricks in buildings exploded during the Roman Empire, to the point that some towns, such as the coastal settlement of Ostia, were built almost entirely of brick. Not only were towns like Ostia full of brick buildings, they were full of elaborate ornamental brickwork: a sure sign of skilled masons at work.

In addition to laying bricks, masons are also called upon to lay various kinds of tiles. One of the oldest types of tiling materials is called terracotta, which is fired, unglazed clay, reddish-brown in color. It's still used today. The oldest examples of terracotta tiles date to between 2600 and 2000 BCE.

Byzantine Bricklaying Standards

In 330 CE, Emperor Constantine moved his capital from Rome to Constantinople (today's Istanbul), founding the Eastern Roman Empire, otherwise known as the Byzantine Empire. One of the earliest mentions of professional standards for masons comes from the Byzantine Empire, from *The Book of Eparch*, which records details about trade guilds in Constantinople in the tenth century CE.

The Book of Eparch states that builders were only allowed to work on one project at a time. For any brick buildings they constructed, they remained accountable for faults for ten years. It includes this note specific to bricklayers: "Those who build walls and domes or vaults of brick must possess great exactitude and experience lest the foundation prove unsound and the building crooked or uneven."

That remains as true today as it was then.

Medieval Masonry

Masons were highly regarded during medieval times: they were the skilled craftsmen who built castles, churches, and cathedrals, primarily with stone, but also with brick. The work of stonemasons can be seen in the Egyptian pyramids, Greek temples, and Roman amphitheaters, but their heyday was undoubtedly the Middle Ages, when they built thousands of castles and churches across western Europe in the eleventh and twelfth centuries alone.

All stonemasonry begins with the ability to cut a flat surface in a piece of stone, and all that takes is a mallet, a chisel, and a metal straight edge. The tools used today are virtually unchanged from the tools of yesteryear: chisels found at the pyramids of Giza come in the same range of shapes and sizes as chisels today.

Unlike brick masons, stonemasons often sign their work, carving a personal symbol, called a Banker Mark, into the stones they use. Some of these marks have been in use within families for many generations.

Like other medieval craftsmen, masons belonged to a guild. Guilds were organizations to which anyone practicing a specific craft had to belong if they wanted to work in a town. The guilds paid a license fee to the city or local ruler. In exchange for holding a monopoly on its particular craft, each guild would regulate the quality of work its members provided and make sure they held up their end of contracts. Guilds also offered other services, such as taking care of members suffering from poor financial or physical health and looking after the widows of members killed while on the job.

Most guilds were linked to particular towns, but not the masons' guild: it was international, because masons were in such demand, they would move from town to town as needed.

In some towns, where a shortage of stone resulted in more bricklaying, there might be a separate bricklayers' guild, but in places where there was a lot of stone—Oxford, England, for instance—the bricklayers would be part of the masons' guild. That was usually the case in smaller towns, too.

Within the guild, a mason would begin as an apprentice. After seven or eight years, he would become a journeyman. (Although journeymen traveled to find work, the name probably comes from the French word *jour*, meaning "day," because a journeyman would be paid by the day.) Finally, a journeyman would become a master mason and take on apprentices himself. Even today, some elements of this system remain.

INDUSTRIAL BRICKMAKING AND PORTLAND CEMENT

For centuries, masons constructed amazing works of brick and stone all over the world, from China to the Middle East to Europe to, eventually, the New World. During the Renaissance, enormously skilled stonemasons built structures we continue to admire for their artistry today, including more cathedrals, beautiful fountains, and many other buildings. Brickmaking, too, continued to evolve. Like other industries, it became mechanized in the nineteenth century, during the Industrial Revolution, with dozens of machines for making bricks patented and new methods of firing bricks developed as well.

Another new form of technology also appeared. On October 21, 1824, bricklayer Joseph Aspdin of Leeds, England, took out a patent on a new artificial stone, which he called Portland Cement because it was white, like Portland stone. (The ancient Romans had a form of cement, but it was brown.) In truth, though, it was his son, William Aspdin, some eighteen years later, who produced true Portland Cement, when he accidentally discovered a way to improve on his father's original recipe.

Today, literal mountains of materials (such as limestone, shells, and chalk) are combined with shale, clay, slate, blast furnace slag, silica sand, and iron ore, heated to a high temperature, and then ground into a fine powder: cement.

Portland Cement like this has now almost entirely replaced the much weaker lime mortar bricklayers have used for centuries.

Portland Cement replaced lime mortar in bricklaying. Lime mortar, made of lime and (typically) sand, mixed with water, had been in use since the fourth century BCE to hold together bricks as well as layers of bricks, but it was relatively weak. Portland Cement mortar is often stronger than the bricks themselves.

Whereas lime mortar allowed bricks to move in relation to each other as they expanded and contracted, Portland Cement mortar glued the bricks together strongly. This required the introduction of special joints, called expansion joints, to allow sections of a wall to expand and contract separately. Otherwise the whole wall would expand and contract, which could break a building apart.

CONCRETE BLOCKS

Later, cement gave rise to concrete, which is made by mixing a paste of Portland Cement and water with fine and coarse aggregates (otherwise known as small and larger rocks). The cement coats the surfaces of the rocks. As the paste hardens, it gains strength, binding the rocks together into a single rock-like mass.

The first hollow concrete block was designed in 1890 by Harmon S. Palmer in the United States. He experimented for ten years before patenting the design in 1900. The idea of using concrete blocks in building took off quickly: by 1905, an estimated 1,500 companies were manufacturing concrete blocks in the United States. Those early blocks, like early bricks, were made by hand: it would take a worker an hour to make ten of them. Today, modern block-making machines turn out up to two thousand an hour.

A mason in Palm Beach, Florida, builds a wall using concrete blocks, the second most common masonry construction material after bricks.

Concrete blocks were first used in the United States as a substitute for stone or wood in the building of homes because it was cheaper than a more traditional wood-framed stone- or brick-clad building. It was particularly popular in the early twentieth century, especially in the Midwest, where the raw materials were abundant. Today, while brick is most commonly used in masonry, the concrete block is close behind it.

Through all these changes in technology and building techniques, one thing has remained constant: the need for masons—people skilled in laying brick and working with stone, tile, and concrete. Although new skills have to be developed as new materials and building processes come along, the occupation itself has remained a constant source of employment for millennia...an unbroken line of artisans in which anyone becoming a mason today can proudly claim membership.

chapter 2

THE ESSENTIAL SKILLS OF MASONRY

If you consult the Merriam-Webster dictionary for a definition of "mason," you'll get a very succinct answer: "a skilled worker who builds by laying units of substantial material (as stone or brick)." Fortunately, a proper definition takes a few more words than that, or this would be a very short section.

There are brick masons, block masons, stonemasons, and refractory masons, as well as masons who specialize in laying tile. As noted in the first section, the most ancient form of masonry is bricklaying. Bricklayers, or brick masons, use bricks to construct a variety of structures, including homes, warehouses, and walls. Block masons work with concrete blocks. Typically, a mason will be both a brick mason and a block mason, so the two terms are often used interchangeably. Jobs are usually supervised by an experienced mason, called either a general or masonry contractor.

LAYING BRICKS, BLOCKS, AND TILES

Masons can work indoors or outdoors, on new construction projects or on existing structures, and on either commercial or residential properties. Whether a project is large or small, masons work with other members of the construction industry. They look at plans or blueprints and determine appropriate

A bricklayer in British Columbia, Canada, applies mortar, the material that binds bricks together, as he builds the wall of a structure.

measurements and what types of materials and labor are required for a project.

Most bricklaying projects begin the same way. The first step in laying bricks or blocks in a vertical structure is to place the bottom layer in what's called "dry course," without any mortar. Traditionally the work begins by building the corners at each end of the structure. These pyramid-shaped structures, called "leads," take meticulous work and are built by the most experienced masons. Because they are difficult to construct, leads are expensive. Instead, many masons use corner poles or guides to show the lines the walls will take as they're erected.

Once the corners are built (or the poles are in place), cords are stretched between them to outline the walls. Using the corner leads or poles and the cords as guides, masons lay the bricks or concrete blocks (generically called "masonry units") in straight, level layers, beginning with a layer of mortar to serve as the base, and following that up with more mortar between individual bricks or blocks and between each layer. Made of cement, sand, and water, mortar must be mixed carefully: learning to mix and spread it is a basic masonry skill.

If a masonry unit is too large for a space, it may be broken with a hammer or cut with a power saw to fit. In general, to make a wall stronger, masons don't lay bricks or blocks so the vertical joints overlap.

Once the wall is built, masons use specific jointing tools to smooth out the mortar to give the bricks a polished, clean look. Masons may also build arches out of brick around openings such as windows and doors.

Masons may also install materials other than bricks and blocks. For instance, high-rise buildings often include large, pre-fabricated insulated wall panels that have to be hoisted into place by a crane, and then bolted or welded to a steel or concrete framework. Positioning the panels is often the work of masons, who may also assist with the welding, if they've

Because it is vital to the structural integrity of any masonry construction, mortar must be carefully mixed. It is a skill most masons learn early in their training.

been trained and certified in that skill.

Some masons are also tile layers. Tile layers make detailed measurements and then lay out tiles on a dry surface. Because tile patterns are often quite complicated, laying them out on a dry surface helps prevent layers from making mistakes. Electric or mechanical tools are used to cut the tiles as necessary to go around pipes and other fixtures. Sometimes drywall will have to be installed for wall tiles, or a concrete floor or other uneven surface may need to be leveled with mortar before the tiles are finally set in mortar themselves. Once the tiles have been set, a pre-seal may have to be applied to unglazed tiles. Finally, grout is applied between the tiles. The excess is wiped away with damp sponges. Once the grout sets, a final sealing agent may need to be applied.

One specialized type of mason is the refractory mason. That might sound like a mason who's hard to get along with, but really it's a mason who specializes in installing special kinds of brick and tile in

The Tools of the Trade

Masonry continues to be a very "hands-on" occupation, and many of the tools used haven't changed much in generations—or centuries.

Here are some common ones:

Trowel: A trowel consists of a handle and, offset below it, a leaf-shaped blade. Trowels are used for spreading mortar, repairing old mortar joints, and scraping off excess mortar.

Mason's hammer: One end of this hammer is square, for hammering nails or anything else that needs hammering. The other end is sharp, like a small chisel, and used to make a cutting line around a block or brick that needs to be split. Once the line is marked with the sharp end, a blow with the hammer end makes the block or brick break cleanly where required.

Blocking chisel: A blocking chisel is a heavy chisel up to eight inches wide (it comes in many sizes and shapes). Made of steel, it's used to split blocks or bricks very cleanly, usually with just one blow of a hammer on its narrow end.

Mashing hammer: This is the tool used to strike the blocking chisel. It has two flat striking ends and is fairly heavy, at between two and four pounds.

Square: Typically made of steel, a square is essentially two rulers joined together at right angles. It's used to make sure wall corners and window and door openings are at right angles.

Jointer: These pieces of shaped metal are used to finish a mortar joint. They're pressed into the mortar joint after it has dried enough to take a fingerprint. There are many different sizes and shapes of jointers.

Before investing in any tools, it is a good idea to get recommendations from seasoned masons on the equipment that is most suited to a particular project.

The trowel, which this bricklayer is using to apply mortar to the bricks of a wall, is one of the most basic—and ancient—tools of the mason.

A mason uses a rubber mallet to tap the tiles he's been laying, ensuring they are well and evenly set in the mortar.

high-temperature environments, such as boilers and industrial furnaces. One common place for refractory masons to work is in steel mills, where molten metal flows along refractory beds.

A still more specialized form of mason is the restoration mason. These masons, also known as Pointer, Cleaner, Caulker (PCC) workers, both fix or finish joints on new masonry (known as pointing), as well as clean, caulk, and weatherproof them, and restore older buildings by caulking, cleaning, weatherproofing, and replacing old mortar. Because older brick buildings continue to age, the need for this type of mason is expected to be high in coming years.

Stonemasonry

Finally, there are the stonemasons. They work with stone rather than brick or blocks, constructing floors, fences, walls, and exteriors, out of both natural cut stone (granite, limestone, marble,

Keeping walls straight both vertically and horizontally is one of the most important tasks of a mason. Here, a mason uses a spirit level to ensure the wall he's building is horizontal.

etc.) and manmade stone or concrete.

Stonemasons often work from special, highly detailed plans, which number each individual stone that will be used in the job. Sometimes these stones are so large and heavy they have to be maneuvered with a crane.

To build a stone wall, a stonemason sets out the first course in a prepared bed of mortar, just like a brick mason. The stonemason then uses wedges, plumb lines, and levelers to set the stones in the straight line, hammering them into place with a heavy rubber mallet. As the wall grows, layer by layer, the mason removes the supporting wedges, fills in any gaps left between the (typically irregularly shaped) stones, and uses yet another specialized tool, known as a "tuck pointer," to even out the surface of the mortar. Sometimes, stonemasons have to bolt large stones to anchors in the wall to keep them in place.

To lay a stone floor, the stonemason first lays a bed of mortar. Floors typically use larger, heavier blocks of stone than walls. The stones are placed using crowbars and mallets. Then the spaces in between them are filled in with mortar and everything is smoothed and cleaned.

Stonemasonry may also involve cutting stone, a difficult task that requires great skill. Stones are cut following the natural grain of the stone using specially constructed hammers and chisels. Large, hard, and valuable pieces of stone may be cut using a special diamond-bladed saw. (Diamond is the hardest known substance.)

Hard Work

Most masonry work is done outside, and it can be physically demanding, since masons have to carry heavy equipment and supplies and stand, stoop, and kneel for long periods of time. Many of the tools used are dangerous, and the environments in which masons work can also be hazardous, so proper safety equipment (such as harnesses when working on tall structures, and eye and ear protection) is important, as is a

A hard hat, goggles, gloves, and clothing that covers arms and legs are some of the safety gear generally required or advised for masons when they are working on a project.

general focus on safety. Safety requirements may vary, depending on where a job is located, but standard safety gear includes a hard hat, goggles, gloves, and protective clothing.

Most masons are men. However, with the support of communities and organizations for tradeswomen, an increasing number of women are overcoming barriers that traditionally prevented them from entering the field, or those that make it difficult for them to advance in the field. Al Herndon, northern apprenticeship representative for Florida Masonry Apprentice and Education Foundation, told *U.S. News & World Report*, "We find that our female masons tend to become very proficient in detail work." But women are not limited to detail work alone. They are bricklayers and stonemasons. They have gone on to reach journeyman status, a goal for any apprentice mason.

For anyone, it's tough, demanding work, but at the end of it, masons can look with pride at something they have constructed with their own hands, something that may stand for years, decades, or even centuries. Very few careers offer that kind of reward.

chapter 3

Training to Become a Mason

You don't have to go to school to become a mason: in fact, most masons enter the job through on-the-job training. They may get hired as a general laborer, begin assisting masons, and then decide to pursue it as a career.

However, formal training is available, through a vocational school or one of many courses provided by the industry. These training programs can begin quite early: many high schools offer vocational-technical (vo-tech) programs in various trades, including bricklaying and other forms of masonry.

High School Programs

There are hundreds of vocational programs in masonry available to high schol students. By way of example, consider the program offered at Choffin Career and Technical Center in Youngstown, Ohio. High school students can attend Choffin full-time or for half-days, maintaining their connections with their regular high schools while training for a trade.

The Choffin program starts with laying brick and block and moves on to building and installing glass block windows. Students learn how to mix concrete and mortar; how to pour concrete for stepping stones, park benches, and bird baths; how to lay paving brick; how to build a fireplace front, turn, and arch; and how to repair brickwork and mortar joints. The

This student is learning how to use a trowel to spread mortar in a bricklaying workshop. Courses and workshops in masonry provide a constructive environment in which to learn basic skills.

course also includes first aid and safety training. There are many other programs available through such organizations or through high schools themselves.

THE INTERNATIONAL MASONRY INSTITUTE

One of the leading providers of masonry training is the International Masonry Institute (IMI), which trains students in the craft and also offers professional education for masonry contractors and free technical assistance to designers and builders.

IMI is a strategic alliance between the International Union of Bricklayers and Allied Craftworkers (BAC) and the union's signatory contractors, designed to promote quality masonry construction. Its team includes architects, engineers, construction managers, skilled craftworkers, and instructors.

The IMI operates a central education facility, the Flynn Center in Fort Ritchie, Maryland, where it trains individuals in brick, stone, and refractory masonry, as well as safety, building scaffolds, and working with terrazzo and tile. The IMI also has a number of regional centers. Details of the IMI's programs can be found at its website, www.imiweb.org.

CERTIFICATION PROGRAMS

At the post–high school level, prospective masons can take a masonry certificate program through a community college, vocational school, or other educational facility. To enroll in most such programs, students need a high school diploma or GED certificate. Good math skills are important: an important aspect of masonry is estimating the cost of labor and materials (and the quantity of materials needed). Masons also have to be able to read construction blueprints and follow structural plans and safety regulations.

Masonry certificate programs generally require two to four semesters of study.

Working with an experienced instructor in a course allows students to make mistakes and learn proper masonry techniques before they tackle a real-world project.

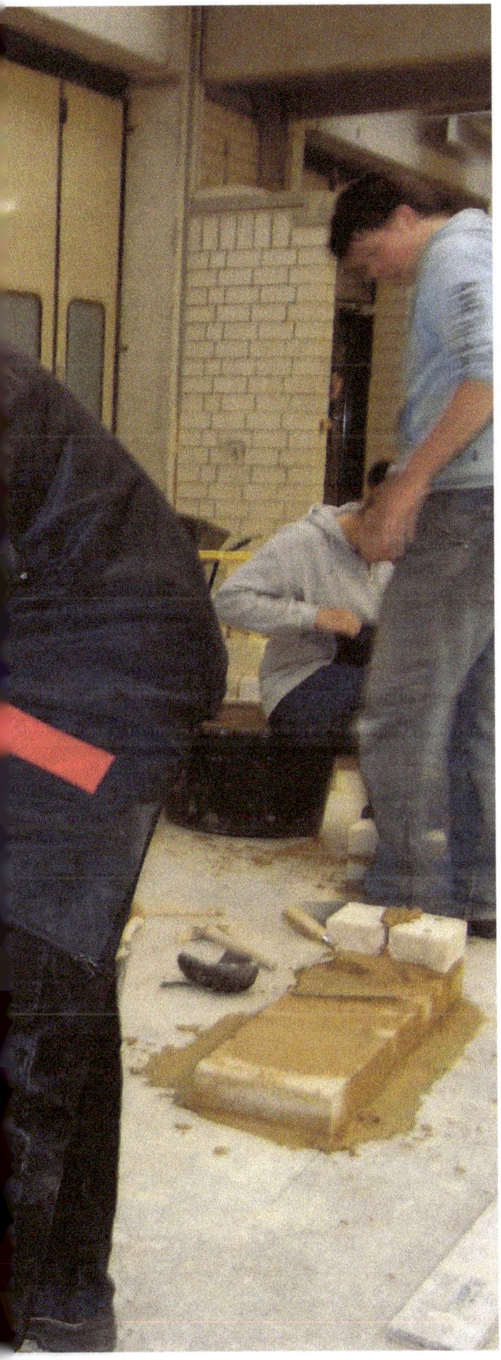

Students learn basic and advanced bricklaying and masonry practices, as well as how to safely build and maintain stone, concrete, and brick structures. They both attend classes and gain hands-on experience. Common courses cover basic bricklaying, masonry processes, reading masonry diagrams and blueprints, cleaning, pointing and caulking, masonry power tools, stonework, and cost estimation.

Students coming out of these courses are in a good position to move into an apprenticeship program. Becoming an apprentice continues to be the main pathway to a full-time career as a mason, just as it has been for hundreds of years.

APPRENTICING AS A MASON

When you become an apprentice mason, you enter into an agreement with an employer. The employer needs a skilled mason and offers an apprentice the opportunity to become one through a combination of classroom learning and on-the-job

Apprentice masons learn on the job, under the supervision of experienced mentors who are usually journeymen. Apprentices work to become journeymen themselves one day.

experience. Different kinds of apprenticeship programs are offered by schools, training centers, unions, and contractors.

Most masonry apprenticeships last three years, although requirements vary among programs. An apprentice will typically complete around 144 hours of classroom instruction, with classes held one or two evenings per week. Classes cover the theoretical and technical aspects of masonry.

Additionally, the apprentice spends around 1,500 hours in on-the-job training, under the supervision of qualified mentors. If you have completed "pre-apprenticeship" courses—such as those offered in high schools—you may be given credit for having already completed some of the necessary apprenticeship training.

One of the great things about apprenticeship training is that you earn while you learn. Apprentices are paid for their on-the-job training, with wages generally beginning at half the salary of a journeyman mason, and rising to up to 90 percent by the final year of training.

Competing Apprentices

Every year ,the Mason Contractors Association of America (MCAA) runs the Masonry Skills Challenge, a competition of masonry apprentices at first-, second-, and third-year skill levels, vying to win the title Best Masonry Apprentice.

Entrants are given a surprise project to complete, appropriate to their skill level. They have three hours to do so with the materials provided, and they can't consult with anyone during those three hours. The MCAA provides judges. Judges look at features such as plumb (how straight a vertical component is), level (how straight a horizontal component is), neatness, measurements, and the overall aesthetics of the project, among other things.

Before competing in the national challenge, contestants must win one of nine regional contests. Many similar competitions are held around the world.

Moreover, if you're apprenticed to a contractor, he or she may cover the classroom tuition as well.

The precise requirements for apprenticeships vary from state to state and region to region. In some places, a high school diploma is required (and it is generally preferred even where it isn't a requirement). The minimum age for apprentices can also vary, but seventeen is fairly typical.

It's very helpful to be comfortable with geometry and algebra, and map, blueprint, or instruction reading, all of which are skills that will be taught in the classroom portion of the apprenticeship. Digital skills may also become important in the future, as computer technology begins to have a greater impact on the trade.

Most apprentices begin by working as a laborer for four or five weeks, transporting supplies, mixing mortar, constructing scaffolding around work sites, and so forth.

Through this process the apprentice learns about the materials, tools, and procedures masons use.

The next step is learning to work with bricks and blocks: laying mortar, cutting, aligning, connecting. During the apprenticeship, apprentices will typically learn how to use stone and concrete as well as brick, so they can be certified in multiple skills.

Daniel O'Shea, who won the Apprentice of the Year award in 2014 for the U.K. homebuilding company Redrow, summed up the apprenticeship process well in an interview with *Housebuilder & Developer* magazine: "Being an apprentice is a real eye opener to the industry. You meet new people, learn new skills and gain an insight into other people's skills as well as your own. And you earn money while you are learning. I love being an apprentice and I'm always encouraging my friends and other students...to follow suit."

Some workers become masons without going through the formal apprenticeship program, although that typically takes longer. Like apprentices, they might begin as laborers or "mason tenders." As they pick up skills informally on the job, they might be promoted to laying stone or brick themselves.

Continuing Education

Masons can continue to develop their skills throughout their career. Many vocational schools offer masonry training workshops addressing specific areas, such as bricklaying, pointing and cleaning, masonry alteration, decorative masonry, or installing firebrick.

Workshops may also be offered by employers, and professional organizations, such as the Mason Contractors Association of America (MCAA), offer online and in-person seminars for masons, mason foremen, and masonry supervisors as part of a continuing education program.

The International Masonry Institute (IMI) is one organization that offers cross-training in a variety of masonry crafts, including brick, tile, terrazzo, marble, stone, plaster, cement, and refractory. It also offers upgrade training in flashing,

There are many types of masons with specialized skills. This stonemason is using a chisel to carve an inscription into a block of stone.

welding, blueprint reading, grout/reinforced masonry and new products, health and safety instruction, and a supervisor certification program for current and future foremen or supervisors.

Just as there are competitions for apprentices, there are competitions for journeyman masons who want to hone their skills in a competitive environment. One well-known competition is the Spec Mix Brick Layer 500 World Championship. It can take years for someone to become an accomplished enough bricklayer to win the contest. In 2015, the event drew nearly four thousand spectators to watch twenty-four competitors from all over the world compete for an hour for the title of World's Best Bricklayer. The winner, Fred Campbell of Tennessee, laid 743 bricks, demonstrating both skill and craftsmanship as he did so. He won a truck and more than $10,000 in cash and prizes.

Campbell also won in 2013. In an interview with *Masonry Magazine* after his first win, he said he was hooked on masonry from the moment he first began laying bricks alongside his father, a life-long mason contractor. "Dad taught me everything he knew and was really strict with me,"

Campbell said. "He always taught me to do a good job and do it like it was your own house. If you would not accept your work on your house, don't expect someone else to accept it that way."

Campbell, now in his mid-forties, took over his father's business when he was just eighteen. He trained or retrained the majority of his employees and believes mentored training—the apprenticeship model—is essential, especially for masons who can move beyond laying bricks and blocks to building fireplaces, chimneys, arches, and other complex decorative elements. "We are really fortunate that we do what we do," Campbell added. "It's a good career choice."

chapter 4

Beyond Apprenticeship

The goal of the apprenticeship program is to become a journeyman. Journeymen are skilled masons who are qualified and free to seek out their own work. Typically they're hired by contractors to work on a specific building project. Some are self-employed or eventually start their own businesses.

Just as there are different specific requirements for apprentices that vary from state to state and region to region, each state or region sets its own requirements for the licensing of building contractors and subcontractors. Some masons may be required to have a license in order to offer their services. A mason who owns a business and contracts directly with clients is almost certainly going to need a license. Masons who subcontract on projects managed by a contractor may have to have a license if the project costs more than a certain set amount. Obtaining a license typically involves passing an exam, submitting financial records, and providing references and proof of insurance.

Masons who own their own company can seek certification from the MCAA. To obtain certification, the owner must attend training courses to earn one hundred educational credits and pass a multiple-choice exam. To renew certification, the owner and supervisors of the company must participate in continuing education courses throughout the three-year certification period, but they do not need to retake the exam.

GETTING WORK

There are many routes to finding jobs. Those who go through apprenticeship programs develop many contacts with

Apprenticeships are a great way to make contacts in the industry and in your area. The individuals you meet may have leads on opportunities for you when your apprenticeship is over.

contractors, masonry companies, and other masons. National associations like the MCAA offer job listings. Even high school programs can open the door to masonry jobs, since they are typically taught by experienced masons who may own their own companies or have connections with contractors looking for workers. Some masons work for unionized companies or on projects that employ only unionized workers. Others work for themselves or for companies that are not unionized.

Once a mason starts working on a particular project, it may keep him or her busy for a long time. Large housing projects and commercial projects may take more than two years to complete. Residential work, on the other hand, tends to be shorter. Masons who work on commercial jobs are usually more experienced and earn higher salaries than residential masons. They also face more workplace regulation and are typically closely overseen by project architects and engineers.

Many masons travel to find work when local work is scarce or not available. "You can go anywhere the job goes," Al Herndon (quoted earlier) told *U.S. News & World Report*. "There are crews that travel and crews that work in

Most major commercial construction projects, like the high-rise building to which this worker is applying plaster, utilize a unionized workforce.

the local area. If you're a traveling mason, you probably do make a little extra money."

The most experienced masons are skilled in working with all forms of structural material, including brick, block, stone, glass, and synthetics. The more materials a mason is capable of working with, the easier it is to find work.

JOINING THE UNION

It's estimated that about 20 percent of masons in the United States are self-employed. Many more are members of the

A UNION CHANGES THE WAY YOU WORK

Bill Toler is one example of a brick mason who has been both nonunionized and unionized. He spent twelve years outside the union before deciding to join the International Union of Bricklayers and Allied Craftworkers. He first had to join an apprenticeship program to "rebuild" himself. He told the McGraw-Hill's College and Career Readiness website that the union changed the way he worked: "When you are a bricklayer outside the union, you may be a construction laborer for a few days and then a brick mason for a few days," he said. "But as a member of the union, you don't cross occupational lines. You're a brick mason every day."

Toler told the website that he thinks being a brick mason offers an important opportunity for young people. Among other things, it teaches discipline in addition to providing a way to earn a living. "Other jobs might permit disorganization—you might be late to work, for example. Not bricklaying. There are other guys out there wanting your job, so you've got to be the best. You've got to be on top of your game all the time."

He also notes that there's always something new to learn—and best of all, at the end of a job, there's something permanent you can look at and think, *I built that.*

International Union of Bricklayers and Allied Craftworkers (BAC). Founded in 1865, BAC is the oldest continuous union in North America. It represents the most highly skilled masons across the United States and Canada, including bricklayers, stone and marble masons, cement masons, plasterers, tile setters, terrazzo and mosaic workers, and pointers/cleaners/caulkers. BAC offers a variety of benefits to its members,

Erecting scaffolding is an example of a task that might be done by a mason on a non-unionized job but will probably be done by a general laborer on a unionized one.

including pension and health benefits and a job network (a bulletin board–style system where job opportunities are posted when there is a shortage of workers in a specific area), among numerous others.

Many masons find it beneficial to belong to the union. Audon Edgar Morales, an experienced mason, told the newspaper *South Coast Today* that he made $27 an hour before joining the union, and $49 an hour afterward. On the other hand, he noted, he now spends three or four months of the year unemployed, whereas he worked year round before joining the union.

For Morales, the biggest change was the work environment. He said in the union there was more respect for the workers. "When you do your eight hours, and you go home, you get out more relaxed mentally," he said. "When I was [not in the union], I felt depressed because of the way we were treated."

Unionized masons, however, typically don't have the opportunity to undertake as wide a variety of tasks as non-unionized masons. Crafts are defined under collective bargaining agreements: a mason might be limited to tasks like cutting bricks and laying grout, whereas laborers would be responsible for scaffolding and tending to the mortar.

In the same article in the *South Coast Today* newspaper, Victor Fernandes, who with his three brothers owns Fernandes Masonry, a non-union company with up to 120 employees at any one time, noted that his employees could be working on a wall one minute, then putting up scaffolding, then picking up mortar. "If you join you can't do that," Fernandes said. "The jobs are all split up."

In the end, each mason has to decide for him- or herself whether joining the union is the best choice.

chapter 5

THE FUTURE OF MASONRY

Whenever the economy takes a turn for the worse, jobs are lost or harder to come by. That's as true of masons as it is for any other occupation. But it's also true that a weak economy affects the prospects for skilled masons less than some other occupations.

In fact, the US Bureau of Labor Statistics projects that employment of brick masons, block masons, and stonemasons will grow 34 percent from 2012 to 2022, much faster than the average for all occupations. The reason? Population growth is expected to result in the construction of more schools, hospitals, apartment buildings, and other structures—and, of course, schools, hospitals, apartment buildings, etc., use lots of brick, block, or stone. Brick and stone exteriors can be expensive, but they remain popular because they are low-maintenance and durable. And it's not just new buildings that will provide jobs. Many existing brick buildings are aging, which means there is an ongoing need for masons capable of repairing and restoring them.

Repair and reconstruction of aging structures will provide many jobs for masons in the future. These skilled masons are carefully reconstructing a wall, using the original stones as much as possible.

In areas prone to hurricanes, building codes increasingly require durable homes made of brick, block, or stone. Moreover, the areas prone to hurricanes are also areas with otherwise generally good climates, where masons can work year-round, rather than seasonally.

The current masonry workforce is growing older, and many workers are expected to retire over the next decade, which will create some job openings. The number of jobs opening up from employment growth is expected to be much greater.

So the jobs will be there. But will the work of masons continue to look the same in the future as it does today?

COMPUTER SKILLS

Although traditionally computer skills wouldn't be considered an important aspect of being a successful mason, that may change in the future. One of the new technologies sweeping the construction industry is something called building information modeling (BIM). This is a computerized process for modeling buildings and planning their construction.

BIM isn't new to the construction industry, but the masonry trade has lagged behind some of the others, such as concrete placement and steel, in making good use of it. David Biggs, who teaches historic preservation engineering at the University of Pennsylvania, told *Masonry Magazine* that if the masonry industry doesn't incorporate BIM technology, masonry as a construction method may

The use of computers for modeling buildings and planning their construction before they are built is changing the way masons work and will have an increasing impact in the future.

come to be seen as difficult to work with, and therefore uncompetitive. "It is no doubt the future of masonry. It's not a choice, but a must," Biggs said. Biggs is program coordinator of BIM for Masonry Initiative, which represents the masonry industry of the United States and parts of Canada, and promotes the development of techniques and tools to assist designers, manufacturers, contractors, construction managers, and owners in the better use of masonry with BIM technology.

BIM uses 3D computer modeling to create digital models of buildings, from the interior to the exterior. This makes the scheduling, estimating, site planning and record-keeping in construction trades more accurate. All of the information can be accessed and shared interactively with everyone from architects to craftworkers, such as masons.

As the masonry industry moves into the future, then, masons who are as comfortable with computer technology as they are with trowels, chisels, and mallets may have an advantage. And even as the computer revolution is just beginning to make itself felt in the masonry industry, there's another revolution that could have even farther-reaching consequences: robotics.

Developments in Robotics

A number of machines for automating portions of masonry work are in development. The most complete—it is just about ready to enter the work force in a big way—is called SAM (Semi-Automated Masonry).

SAM was first proposed in 2007 by Nathan Podkaminer, a registered architect with more than forty years of experience who has managed several multimillion dollar construction projects. He felt a bricklaying robot could help masonry retain its position as the preferred method of building walls. In conjunction with inventor and entrepreneur Scott L. Peters, he founded Construction Robotics.

There were still missing technologies, however. Robots are typically designed for use in a controlled environment. They're often bolted to the concrete floor of a factory. Using a robot on an ever-changing construction site—about as far from a controlled environment as it's possible to get—posed a problem.

"The human brain is incredible and it's challenging to replicate accurately what a bricklayer does," Podkaminer said in an interview with the *Journal of Commerce*. "A human bricklayer adjusts instantaneously for wind, other workers on the scaffold and other conditions. It took us two years just to perfect SAM's ability to extrude mortar onto a brick."

The prototype version of SAM was launched in 2011, and proved feasible during a test on an actual jobsite. Further development followed. By 2014, a new,

An Earlier Attempt at Automation

SAM is hardly the first attempt to use automation to deal with the challenges of masonry. On January 18, 1918, an inventor named Jasper N. Youngblood filed a patent for a "bricklaying machine."

In his application, he wrote:

"This invention aims to provide a simple means whereby brick may be taken up, transported to a wall, and laid in the wall, mortar being deposited on each course, and the mortar being troweled off and smoothed down, to make a good bed for the next succeeding course of brick."

It never took off—not surprising considering the challenges the developers of SAM have faced even with modern technology. Instead, most improvements in the industry have been focused on the manufacturing side of the process—better methods for drying, firing, and handling brick—rather than on the construction side.

improved SAM was ready for testing. Its first assignment was on a five-story barracks project at Fort Lee, Virginia, where it worked alongside masons from Manning Construction.

Once SAM was set up for a section of wall, the operator ran a calibration process that ensured the bricks would be placed where they were supposed to be placed (a rather important detail). That took about five minutes. Then the operator activated the robot, which proceeded to

Robots are finding more and more uses in the masonry industry. Here, robots stack newly sliced bricks at the Acme Brick Co. manufacturing facility in Leeds, Alabama.

continuously lay the wall. SAM was able to lay about two thousand bricks in an eight-hour day.

Mike Manning, the company president, told the *Journal of Commerce* workers treated SAM like an apprentice bricklayer. "We gave them a lot of suggestions on how the system could be made more usable to a masonry contractor," Manning said, but overall, he liked what he saw. "I think it's going to be a great thing for the industry."

The production version of the robot, scheduled to be released in 2016, will be about nine feet wide, four feet tall and 3.5 feet deep, and weigh under 2,000 pounds. That means it can be easily moved from flatbed to worksite using a forklift. Its relative portability means one masonry crew will be able to prepare a section of wall while another crew runs SAM in another location.

In 2015, it was announced in Australia that Hadrian, another bricklaying robot, could build an entire house in two days. It can lay one thousand bricks per hour—faster than SAM and about twenty times faster than a human bricklayer. This robot is able to process information from a 3D computer model of a building. This data tells the robot where the bricks should be placed. It is anticipated that a commercial version of the robot, scheduled to be ready in 2016, will help create jobs in masonry for individuals interested in robotics.

SAM and other robotic bricklayers are expected to cut costs, reduce physical strain and risk of injury for masons on the job, and improve quality. They will also increasingly be tied into the BIM computerized building design process, allowing for better planning and more streamlined construction activity.

What these robots won't do is put masons out of work. Each SAM, for example, requires three people to support it: the operator, a tender (who feeds in bricks and mortars), and a mason, who fastens wall ties, cleans up excess mortar, and fine-tunes minor variances. Rather than eliminate the workforce, it will supplement it. That's a good thing, since there is a shortage of bricklayers.

Today, a mason contractor with an eleven-man crew may lay only two thousand to three thousand bricks during a day's work. The same-size crew could supervise four SAM units, and lay more than eight thousand bricks in a day. Productivity gains like that would allow the mason contractor to work on more jobs simultaneously and lower the installed cost of brick, which would benefit the masonry industry. Growing the industry would mean growing the number of available jobs. In addition to increasing productivity and efficiency, technology like BIM, SAM, and Hadrian may well draw more young, educated, and technically skilled people into the masonry industry.

Sustainability in Masonry

Another promising aspect of masonry is its role in green construction. The durability of masonry materials—including brick, block, stone, and tile—means that structures made from those materials often last for many years and require little repair and replacement. Additionally, very little waste is produced in the manufacture of many masonry materials. When they are produced, bricks and other materials are environmentally safe and they are usually energy efficient materials that insulate well. And even if these materials no longer serve a purpose in one project, they can be reused in others.

Masonry affords flexibility in design and longevity of construction, which goes hand in hand with the goals of environmental sustainability. It is also fairly simple to maintain, which is another goal. As more companies and individuals gravitate toward green construction, masons are likely to continue to play a significant role.

Other Jobs in the Industry

Many masons eventually move beyond simply laying brick or block to other jobs within the masonry industry. The MCAA lists many different career possibilities. Among them are:

Estimator: This is someone who estimates how much of various materials are needed for a job and how many workers and how much time will be needed to use those materials to complete the job. Estimators often use specialized software that helps them make accurate estimations.

Instructor: An instructor is usually a more experienced mason who teaches a new generation of mason apprentices.

Despite the increasing use of robots in the masonry industry, humans will continue to be required for many building tasks.

Jobsite supervisor: This role requires an individual to directly supervise and coordinate the activities of workers and their helpers. Like the master masons of medieval times, the most experienced masons may move on to become supervising journeymen and apprentices.

Project manager: This is someone who plans, directs, coordinates, or budgets all the activities concerned with building and maintaining structures, facilities, and systems.

For those with the skills and will to work, masonry can be an exciting and growing career—and one that may see many exciting developments in the years ahead as technology advances. Yet whatever the changes in technology—and whatever the state of the economy—the world will always need masons, just as it has for thousands of years.

glossary

aggregate Loose particle-like materials, such as sand, gravel, or pebbles, added to a cementing agent to make concrete, mortar, plaster, etc.

apprentice Someone who is employed at low wages learning a particular set of skills under the guidance of a more experienced worker.

archaeologist Someone who studies ancient and recent human past by examining objects from the relevant eras.

bricklayer A worker skilled in working and building structures with bricks.

caulking Both the process and material used to seal joints or seams against leaks.

chisel A metal tool with a flat, sharp end, used to cut and shape a solid material.

contractor Any organization or individual that contracts with another organization or individual for the construction of a building, road, or other project.

craftworker A skilled manual worker trained in a particular craft, such as masonry or plastering.

guild An association of craftworkers who control the practice of their craft, usually within a particular town.

journeyman Someone who has completed an apprenticeship and is fully trained in the set of skills of a particular trade.

laborer A person paid to do unskilled manual work.

medieval The period of European history spanning the fifth to fifteenth centuries, beginning with the collapse of the western Roman Empire and fading into the Renaissance. Also known as the Middle Ages.

mortar Any of various pastelike materials used to bind together bricks or stones.

plumb line A small, heavy object attached to a string or rope, used especially to see if something (such as a wall) is perfectly vertical.

pointing The external part of mortar joints and the repair of gaps in that mortar (more properly called "repointing").

refractory A substance that is resistant to heat.

stonemason A person skilled in working with and building things out of stone.

terracotta A type of fired earthenware ceramic that is light and porous when unglazed.

union An organization of workers formed to protect the rights and interests of its members.

vocational training Education aimed at developing the skills for a particular occupation.

for more information

Associated Builders and Contractors, Inc. (ABC)
440 1st Street, NW
Suite 200
Washington, DC 20001
(202) 595-1505
Website: http://www.abc.org
ABC is a national trade organization of the construction industry. Membership is comprised of individuals representing all specialties of the construction industry. ABC works to ensure that construction work is done safely and ethically while remaining profitable.

Associated General Contractors of America (AGC)
2300 Wilson Boulevard, Suite 300
Arlington, VA 22201
(703) 548-3118
Website: https://www.agc.org
The AGC is represents thousands of firms, individual general contractors, and service providers and suppliers in the construction industry. The organization also provides information on education, training, scholarships, and other resources.

Canada Masonry Centre
360 Superior Boulevard
Mississauga, ON L5T 2N7
Canada
(905) 564-6622
Website: http://www.canadamasonrycentre.com
This is Canada's nationwide organization for masonry

contractors. Its website is a hub for contractors, designers, and others working in the industry.

Canadian Concrete Masonry Producers Association
PO Box 1345
1500 Avenue Road
Toronto, ON M5M 3X0
Canada
(888) 495-7497
Website: http://www.ccmpa.ca
This Canada-wide body works on behalf of concrete masonry producers.

International Masonry Institute
17101 Science Drive
Bowie, MD 20715
(800) 803-0295
Website: http://www.imiweb.org
The International Masonry Institute offers quality training for craftworkers, professional education for masonry contractors, and free technical assistance to the design and construction communities.

The International Union of Bricklayers & Allied Craftworkers
620 F Street NW
Washington, DC 20004
(888) 880-8222
Website: http://www.bacweb.org
Founded in 1865, the International Union of Bricklayers & Allied Craftworkers represents the most highly skilled trowel trades craftworkers across the United States and Canada.

Mason Contractors Association of America
1481 Merchant Drive
Algonquin, IL 60102
(800) 536-2225
Website: http://www.masoncontractors.org
Founded in 1950, the MCAA is the national trade association representing mason contractors. It also provides continuing education, advocates for fair codes and standards, fosters safe work environments, recruits future manpower, and markets the benefits of masonry materials.

The Masonry Foundation
1481 Merchant Drive
Algonquin, IL 60102
(800) 536-2225
Website: http://www.masonryfoundation.org
The Masonry Foundation provides high-quality education, conducts research for the industry, promotes masonry careers, provides grants, and conducts other industry activities.

Masonry Institute of America (MIA)
1315 Storm Parkway
Torrance, CA 90501
(310) 257-9000
Website: https://www.masonryinstitute.org
MIA is a technical and research organization that disseminates information about the masonry industry and is active in developing national building codes, promoting innovation in masonry, and may other endeavors.

The Masonry Society
105 South Sunset Street, Suite Q
Longmont, CO 80501

(303) 939-9700
Website: http://www.masonrysociety.org
The Masonry Society is an international gathering of people interested in the art and science of masonry whose mission is to advance the knowledge of masonry.

National Association of Women in Construction (NAWIC)
327 S. Adams Street
Fort Worth, TX 76104
(817) 877-5551
Website: http://www.nawic.org
The NAWIC provides a host of resources for women in the field of construction. Opportunities for professional development, networking, education, training, and more are available through the organization, which seeks to give voice to the small but growing number of women in construction.

WEBSITES

Because of the changing nature of Internet links, Rosen Publishing has developed an online list of websites related to the subject of this book. This site is updated regularly. Please use this link to access the list:

http://www.rosenlinks.com/ECAR/Mason

for further reading

Campbell, James W. P., and William Pryce. *Brick: A World History.* London, England: Thames & Hudson, 2003.

Cartwright, Peter. *Bricklaying.* New York, NY: McGraw-Hill Education, 2002.

Cramb, Ian. *The Art of the Stonemason.* Chambersburg, PA: Alan C. Hood & Co, 2006.

Collinson, Jon. *Brickwork and Bricklaying: A DIY Guide.* Ramsbury, England: The Crowood Press, 2012.

Glass, Carter. *The Complete Guide to Ceramic Tile.* Minneapolis, MN: Creative Publishing International, 2010.

Hall, William. *Brick.* London, England: Phaidon Press, 2015.

Hill, Peter, and John David. *Practical Stone Masonry.* New York, NY: Routledge, 2015.

Hodge, J. C., and Malcolm Thorpe. *Brickwork for Apprentices.* New York, NY: Routledge, 2006.

Kreh, Richard T. *Masonry Skills.* Independence, KY: Cengage Learning, 2014.

Leavitt, Amie Jane. *The Vo-Tech Track to Success in Architecture and Construction.* New York, NY: Rosen Publishing, 2014.

Lemmer, Tom. *Black & Decker: The Complete Guide to Masonry & Stonework.* Minneapolis, MN: Creative Publishing International, 2010.

Niver, Heather Moore. *Careers in Construction.* New York, NY: Rosen Publishing, 2014.

Schmidt, Phil. *Guide to Concrete: Masonry and Stucco Projects.* Minneapolis, MN: Creative Publishing International, 2008.

Wolny, Philip. *High-Risk Construction Work: Life Building Skyscrapers, Bridges, and Tunnels.* New York, NY: Rosen Publishing, 2009.

bibliography

The Brick Directory. "The History of Bricks." Retrieved July 8, 2015 (http://www.brickdirectory.co.uk/html/brick_history.html).

Bureau of Labor Statistics. "Brickmasons, Blockmasons, and Stonemasons." United States Department of Labor. Retrieved May 30, 2015 (http://www.bls.gov/ooh/construction-and-extraction/brickmasons-blockmasons-and-stonemasons.htm).

Campbell, James W. P., and William Pryce. *Brick: A World History*. London, England: Thames & Hudson, 2003.

Career Center. "Brick Mason: Training and Education." McGraw-Hill Education College & Career Readiness. Retrieved May 15, 2015 (http://ccr.mcgraw-hill.com/2011/07/23/brick-mason/).

Construction Opportunities Development Council. "Bricklayer/Tilesetter." Retrieved May 30, 2015 (http://www.codc.ca/careers/building-trades/bricklayer-tilesetter/).

HbD Staff. "Award-Winning Apprentices Build Homes and Careers with Redrow." *Housebuilder & Developer*, September 30, 2014. Retrieved May 2, 2015 (http://www.hbdonline.co.uk/news/award-winning-apprentices-build-homes-and-careers-with-redrow/).

Inglesby, Tom. "Going Green: Behind the Scenes." *Masonry Magazine*, November 2006. Retrieved June 10,

2015 (http://www.masonrymagazine.com/11-06/green.html).

Kenter, Peter. "Bricklaying Robot Readied for Work." *Journal of Commerce*, March 30, 2015. Retrieved May 20, 2015 (http://journalofcommerce.com/Technology/News/2015/3/Bricklaying-robot-readied-for-work-1006579W/).

Masonry for Life Staff. "Masonry Basics." Retrieved May 9, 2015 (http://www.masonryforlife.com/HowToBasics.htm).

Morrell, Jennifer. "Masonry and BIM: The Next Level." *Masonry Magazine*, January 2013. Retrieved May 8, 2015 (http://www.masonrymagazine.com/masonry-and-bim-the-next-level/).

Nield, David. "Brick-Laying Robot Can Build House in Two Days." *Gizmag*, June 30, 2015. Retrieved July 8, 2015 (http://www.gizmag.com/hadrian-brick-laying-robot-fastbrick/38239/).

PCA Staff. "How Cement Is Made." Retrieved May 7, 2015 (http://www.cement.org/cement-concrete-basics/how-cement-is-made).

Peters, Scott, and Bob Belden "SAM, the Robotic Bricklayer," *SMART: Dynamics of Masonry*. Retrieved June 4, 2015 (http://www.dynamicsofmasonry.com/content/sam-robotic-bricklayer).

Rios, Simón. "In the Fight for Jobs, Bricklayers' Unions Keep Watchful Eye on Competition." *South Coast Today*,

August 24, 2014. Retrieved May 9, 2015 (http://www.southcoasttoday.com/article/20140824/news/408240322).

Ross, Shelley. "Fred Campbell Is 'World's Best Bricklayer.'" *Masonry Magazine*, April 2013. Retrieved May 4, 2015 (http://www.masonrymagazine.com/fred-campbell-is-worlds-best-bricklayer/).

Salisbury Cathedral Staff . "The History of Stonemasonry." Retrieved May 3, 2015 (http://www.salisburycathedral.org.uk/conservation-restoration-stonemasonry/history-stonemasonry).

Study.com. "Masonry Training Programs and Requirements." Retrieved June 3, 2015 (http://study.com/masonry_training.html).

U.S. News & World Report Money Staff. "Best Construction Jobs: Brickmason and Blockmason." *U.S. News and World Report.* Retrieved May 1, 2015 (http://money.usnews.com/careers/best-jobs/brickmason-and-blockmason).

index

ABOUT THE AUTHOR

Edward Willett is the author of more than fifty books, both nonfiction and fiction, for children, young adults, and adults. He's written about topics as diverse as the Ebola virus, biopharmaceuticals, the Iran-Iraq War, and Jimi Hendrix. He lives in Regina, Saskatchewan, with his wife (an engineer) and teenage daughter.

PHOTO CREDITS

Cover, p. 1 (figure) Sedlacek/Shutterstock.com; cover, p. 1 (background) photosthai/Shutterstock.com; p. 4 © iStockphoto.com/strathroy; p. 8 Matthew M. Schoenfelder/ Lonely Planet Images/Getty Images; p. 10 DEA/G. Dagli Orti/De Agostini/Getty Images; p. 12 Cosmin Sava/ Shutterstock.com; pp. 16-17 Shcherbakov Ilya/ Shutterstock.com; pp. 18-19 Tetra Images/Getty Images; pp. 22, 27 Chris Cheadle/All Canada Photos/Getty Images; pp. 24-25 Eag1eEyes/Shutterstock.com; pp. 28-29 Yunava1/Shutterstock.com; pp. 30-31, 32-33 Reza Estakhrian/Iconica/Getty Images; p. 36 Peter Muller/ Cultura/Getty Images; pp. 38-39 ullstein bild/Getty Images; pp. 40-41 Hybrid Images/Cultura/Getty Images; pp. 44-45 © iStockphoto.com/vallefrias; pp. 48-49 © iStockphoto.com/SolStock; p. 50 Dmitry Kalinovsky/ Shutterstock.com; pp. 52-53 © iStockphoto.com/hxdbzxy; pp. 54-55 David Boyer/National Geographic Image Collection/Getty Images; pp. 56-57 teekid/E+/Getty Images; pp. 60-61 Bloomberg/Getty Images; pp. 64-65 Portland Press Herald/Getty Images

Designer: Matt Cauli; Editor: Shalini Saxena; Photo Researcher: Carina Finn